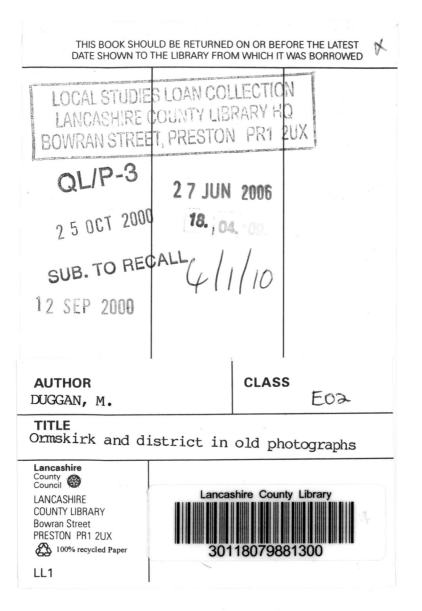

BRITAIN IN OLD PHOTOGRAPHS

ORMSKIRK & DISTRICT

A SECOND SELECTION

MONA DUGGAN

SUTTON PUBLISHING LIMITED

Sutton Publishing Limited
Phoenix Mill · Thrupp · Stroud
Gloucestershire · GL5 2BU

First published 1999

Photograph page 1: Looking towards
Ormskirk Church from Coronation Park in
the 1930s, before the Baths complex was
built.

British Library Cataloguing in Publication Data
A catalogue record for this book is available from the
British Library.

ISBN 0-7509-1935-3

Typeset in 10.5/13.5 Photina.
Typesetting and origination by
Sutton Publishing Limited.
Printed in Great Britain by
Ebenezer Baylis, Worcester.

07988130

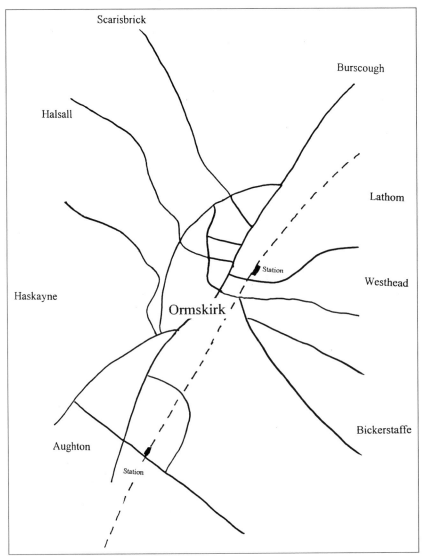

Ormskirk and district.

CONTENTS

A beautiful view of St Michael's Church, Aughton, *c.* 1900. The old man with a scythe was John Hodge, the sexton, who was used as the model for St Peter in one of the windows in the church. Here he symbolises Father Time at work in Ormskirk and District.

INTRODUCTION

This collection of old photographs is a book of memories, some as vivid as if the events happened only yesterday, and others so remote from today that they are only memories of what grandparents had been told. Nevertheless they all form part of the history of the district and should be recorded for posterity. So much has disappeared from both the town and the countryside that it is sometimes hard to recall exactly where old landmarks were located or where once popular shops were situated.

When events and people from the past are remembered, they automatically bring other facts to mind. For instance, the photograph of Latham Hall on page 72 evokes thoughts about that other Lathom House where Lady Charlotte de Tremouille, Lady Derby, defied the Parliamentarian troops and defended her home from 25 February until 26 May 1644. After a second siege the following year, most of the building was demolished, and when the Eighth Earl of Derby returned after the Restoration of Charles II in 1660, he faced the daunting task of rebuilding his home. In 1724 the house passed into the hands of Thomas Bootle of Melling and in 1734 the house in the photograph was completed under the direction of the architect Giacomo Leoni.

The photograph of the church with eighteenth-century windows on page 6 recalls the many restorations which the vicar and the churchwardens supervised over the years as the church moved from a small chapel in the twelfth century to the majestic Victorian church we know today. One restoration followed a disaster in 1724 when the north pillars were 23 inches out of square and one of the beams fell during the morning service, leaving the congregation 'terribly affrighted'. Then another occurred in 1784 when the spire blew down and had to be replaced. We remember the many vicars who served the parish church: John Broxopp who in 1633 refused to wear his surplice on principle, Nathaniel Heywood who in 1662 was ejected for his beliefs, and Zachary Taylor who in 1691 indulged in a war of pamphlets against those who held different opinions to his own.

The various pictures of Ormskirk clock tower, built in 1875 and paid for by public subscription together with the remaining funds of the old court leet, recall the old manor court. That group of voluntary officials administered the town for many centuries when it was one of the manors belonging to Lord Derby. They decided where the market was to be held, they punished those who let their property fall into disrepair, they maintained the quality of goods for sale in the town, and penalised those who committed offences against the general welfare of the town.

To move to more recent times, the photographs of the countryside around Ormskirk evoke another way of life. The harvest relied on the work of man and horse, and the wind was the chief source of power for grinding the corn and grain. Crowds of people responded to the need for seasonal workers when the harvest demanded it, and those same people were ready to dress up in all their finery to celebrate the various festivals, or to grab the opportunity of a coach trip to the seaside.

Several of these photographs are faded and are not as distinct as those taken nowadays, but allowances must be made for their age and for the fact that some of them were taken from newsprint. Similarly some of the names are missing and others may not be correct, but these defects must be attributed to the tricks played by old memories. In the days when these delightful pictures were taken there were no computers to record the facts accurately, so please forgive the shortcomings of the collection and enjoy your trip back to the landscapes and lives of long ago.

The parish church, vicarage and cottages. This view was taken before the great 'restoration' of the church in 1887 when the clock was on the steeple, not on the tower as it is today, the new porch had not been built and the Georgian windows were still in place.

CHAPTER ONE

SHOPS & BUSINESSES

One of the earliest photographs of a shop in Ormskirk. I wonder if it could be the original Mawdsley's shop in Aughton Street or perhaps Wignall's in Church Street, which was mentioned in the 1881 census. Unfortunately no one has been able to identify it. It is interesting to note how specialised the shops in Ormskirk were in those days. Nowadays the sale of china tea would not be sufficiently important to warrant advertising it on the facia board over a shop.

Gilbert's drapery shop at 10 Moor Street. This business remained in the Gilbert family from 1861 to 1881 and continued until this photograph was taken in the early twentieth century. In 1881 William Gilbert aged 28, woollen draper, his brother John aged 23, also a woollen draper, his sister Esther aged 30, a milliner, and his younger sister Mary aged 25, also a milliner, were all employed in the shop. Through the archway was 'Gilbert's Yard', a courtyard development which was home to seven households or thirty-two individuals in 1861.

Robert Lee outside his shop in Aughton Street. His 'china warehouse' was known affectionately as 'Muggy Lee's' until recent times.

Johnson's butcher's shop at 26 Aughton Street. This shop, on the site of Safeway's supermarket, was faced with sandstone blocks which were later covered with mosaic tiles, and the name below the window was painted in gold leaf. The wooden canopy, similar to that over Scott's butcher's shop in Church Street, provided shade over the meat. The smaller carcasses were spring lambs slaughtered for the Easter trade. Standing outside the shop is Jack Johnson, the tallest butcher, no relation to the proprietor, G.A. Johnson.

Mr and Mrs Jones outside their sewing machine shop in Burscough Street.

The fair in the early twentieth century. In 1286 the canons of Burscough Priory were granted the right to hold a fair in Ormskirk in August and in 1461 that was extended to a second fair at Whitsuntide. At first these were primarily for the sale of animals, but later other stalls and entertainments were added. In 1714 Nicholas Blundell actually saw 'a tiger, a civet cat etc' and a 'woman dancing with swords and tankards' at Ormskirk fair. During the Victorian era many of these stalls were abandoned, and the fair reverted to an animal sale.

Moor Street, early 1900s. It is interesting to see the old Ship inn with a gable fronting the street and next to it the property with the Georgian roof-line which was later altered into the new Ship inn with a second gable – the roof-line we know today.

Wainwright's shop adjacent to the King's Arms in Moor Street. The passage at the side of the hotel led into a large stable yard, where riders could leave their horses temporarily while they continued their journey on a fresh horse. Similarly carriage horses could be stabled overnight. Here Peter and Annie Harvey in the trap are preparing to deliver milk from their own cows in Moor Street. Later they opened a fish and chip shop in Aughton Street.

Two young men of the town in the 1920s. Behind them are the stalls erected ready for the market traders to arrive with their wares. The notice on the left shows that Ablett's shoe shop had moved into Moor Street by that time, while another sign at the side of the alleyway announced that next door, Mr Webster of the Ship Inn was offering beer and stout for sale, and also that stabling was available in the yard at the back of that inn.

Mr Ernie Smith and his assistant delivering provender from his shop in Church Street.

Mr Woods, with his wife Ellen and their two daughters Jane and Elizabeth, outside their home at 64 Burscough Street, 1905. The Woods family were ropemakers in Ormskirk for several generations. In the past ropemaking was a very important industry in the district; in fact several of the straight alleyways now in the town originated as ropewalks. The family certainly protected their privacy with shutters, blinds, net curtains and heavy curtains all at that one window.

Bath Spring Brewery. Ellis Ward's brewery developed on the site of an old spring which had been used in the early eighteenth century to provide water for a bathing spa developed by Charles Stanley, cousin of the Earl of Derby, to cater for the emergent fashion of bathing in cold water. The springs around Ormskirk had the reputation of being very beneficial to health; in fact in 1670 an eminent doctor wrote that Ormskirk people had healthier constitutions than most country people – a good recommendation for Ellis Ward's products.

Collecting water from Bath Spring at the end
of the nineteenth century, many years after
the cold water baths had disappeared, but
before the brewery was built.

Dysons of Halsall delivering bottles of mineral waters to the Swan Hotel, 1930s. The curtain
hanging over the back of the lorry must have been used to keep the rain and dust off the bottles
during transit.

The Swan Hotel before it was modernised in 1894.

Laying sets outside the new Swan Hotel. There was a boxing gym in the right-hand side of the building where several well-known boxers trained, and the large room above it was a very popular venue for dances in the 1930s.

The Stanley Gate at Bickerstaffe with its old sign of the five-barred gate. There have been attempts recently to rename the old inn, but at the moment the traditional name remains the same. The inn was also a working farm until February 1932 when Lord Derby sold it to Greenall's Brewery. The old farm buildings can be seen behind the inn.

Washing day at the Stanley Gate. The ladies hanging out the washing are Miss Birchall, the daughter of the innkeeper, Alice Anderton and Ada Marsh. Miss Birchall and Alice are wearing brats, aprons made from hessian.

The Railway Hotel, Aughton, now the Cockbeck Tavern, early 1900s. The baby carriage with the large wheels was typical of those in use at the turn of the century.

The landlord of the Railway Hotel and his family, 1880s. Thomas Bate, who died in 1895 aged 65, his wife Ann, who died in 1906 aged 71, and their family posed outside the hotel with a sweep and a decorator. Perhaps they were superstitious and thought that including those two tradesmen would bring them luck – as happens at some weddings today – or perhaps they were in the midst of spring cleaning. Certainly the two daughters in their jockey caps (the original baseball caps?) do not intend to work hard in those clothes.

Inside the Blue Bell at Barton. At the back are Bill Aindow, Henry Bradley, Jack Whalley and Tommy Ainscough, and in the front is James Cropper.

The Dog and Gun in Long Lane, Aughton, 1914. Presumably this group is the landlord and his family, and includes the donkey which, no doubt, would have had many uses in those days before motorised transport. There are so many similar photographs from this date that it would seem that a travelling photographer had been in the neighbourhood and had called at several of the local inns to photograph innkeepers' families.

The Stanley Arms near St Michael's Church, Aughton. Whereas then the façade was covered with dark pebbledash with white stonework around the windows, now it is white roughcast with dark window framing. The yard with the building is now a car park and the small garden with the wicket gate is now a garage or store room. Many years ago there was also an alehouse near the church called The Ring o' Bells, but that property was demolished when the churchyard was enlarged.

Draper's old smithy, which stood at the junction of Malt Kiln Lane and Parr's Lane, opposite the sawmill. It has long since been demolished and now all that remains is a huge chestnut tree – possibly the one that can be seen leafless in this view – growing on an enclosed triangle of land at the corner of the lane. It seems that this smithy did indeed stand beneath a spreading chestnut tree.

The general store at Four Lane Ends, Bickerstaffe. Although it had a posting box, this shop kept by Mrs Latham was not a post office. She and her daughter Annie made children's dresses, pillow cases, lace and so on, and sold them along with all kinds of other goods in the shop. Each Thursday she bought a sack of peanuts at the market and sold them at the weekend in small quantities to customers from Ormskirk. They would eat them while they rested on the bench outside the shop. Annie, who later became Mrs Banks, took over the business.

Cammack's shop at the lower end of Aughton Street at the bottom of South Terrace.

Delivering bread to John Rothwell's shop at the corner of Scarisbrick Street. Tasker's bakery and shop were in Sandy Lane, Skelmersdale, and long after this photograph was taken Harold Tasker continued to deliver bread around the neighbourhood. This shop is now the headquarters of the Ormskirk and District Labour Party.

The Morris Dancers' inn at Scarisbrick. This inn was formerly called the Maypole and in the days of horse-drawn traffic it was a very convenient place to stop for a meal on the way to Southport.

Almony Cottage, Lathom Park, when it was a post office.

An early garden centre, Rylance's Nursery on Bold Lane, Aughton, later became Nursery Farm. The Rylance family also had a carpentry business on the same site. After they left, it became the home of the Bate family, who were followed by the Warners, who bred miniature Shetland ponies.

Lifting logs at Draper's sawmill in Parr's Lane, Aughton, 1890s. The chimney-stack marks the site of the steam engine which powered the saws, and the rails along the yard were for wagons which carried the logs into the saw mill. The huge wheels beside Mr Draper give some idea of the size of the timber wagons at that time.

Workers at Draper's sawmill, 1894. Many of the Dutch barns constructed by these men can still be seen in the district. Several members of the family appear in this photograph, including Daniel Draper junior who was a smith, sixth from the left on the back row, and, on the front row, Joseph Draper, also a beekeeper, Robert Draper, the undertaker, Daniel Draper (in the hat), who supervised the making of the barns, and Edward Draper who also acted as the local registrar. The sawmill closed in 1975.

In Bold Lane, Aughton. Both this shop and the police station next door to it have now been converted into private houses. Mr Preston, the 'family grocer', baked bread for sale; in fact the man on the left seems to be holding a baker's shovel, used to take loaves out of the old brick ovens. Mr Preston's horse-drawn delivery van called each day at his customers' houses to deliver bread and groceries. Nowadays those enamelled signs advertising Sunlight Soap and Quaker Oats around the shop doorway are valued highly by collectors. The Abram family later kept this shop.

Church Street, 1950s. This shop and the two either side of it were originally the town hall, which was rebuilt by Lord Derby in 1779. The coat of arms was carved by Benjamin Bromfield of Liverpool and the date of the building is on the rainwater hopper. Originally the upper floor was used for meetings of the manor court and various social occasions, and on the ground floor – then arcaded at the front – were several butchers' stalls. On market days meat was sold beneath the arches.

The clock tower and market, late 1890s. Mawdsley's shop, where Ormskirk gingerbreads were sold, can be seen clearly on Aughton Street.

The market in progress in Aughton Street in the 1950s, soon after the property on the corner of Park Road had been demolished.

The cart which delivered the groceries from Mawdsley's shop. The smartly dressed driver seen here was John Hastings who lived in Park Avenue in the 1920s. It is interesting to read the phone number of the shop on the van, Ormskirk 67. According to an old directory there were only fifty-two phones in Ormskirk in 1902.

Evan Heaton's delivery cart on Southport Road, Scarisbrick. The shop where he sold all kinds of groceries was opposite the Red Lion inn near the canal bridge at Scarisbrick. The Morris Dancers' inn can be seen in the distance.

The smithy on the corner of Smithy Lane facing the Swan Hotel. Mr Kirby, the smith, and his two sons continued working here until the late 1940s. The building in the background was a wheelwright's shop, which has since been converted into a cottage. Residential property has also been built on the site of the smithy and its yard.

Wigan Road, Westhead, with the old smithy in the foreground. This is now the property of Cliff Randall Ltd, joiners and cabinet makers.

Church Street, *c*. 1900. Mansergh's shop in the foreground has rolls of linoleum, probably made in Parbold, propped outside. The lino, the watering cans and piles of barrels indicate what a large range of items was available in that shop. The canopy similar to that over Johnson's butcher's shop, can be seen over (what is now) Scott's shop. Set back between the saddler's and the café on the right of the road was the White Lion, and further up the road can be seen the Snigs Foot – now Disraeli's – which has altered very little since that time.

Celebrating the coronation of George VI, 1937. The confectioner at Dorset's cake shop at 8–10 Church Street, Ormskirk, baked a huge cake and decorated it as a crown. It stood in the window to celebrate the coronation and then it was cut up and sold at 6*d* a pound in aid of the hospital. The staff in their blue overalls with white collars and red rosettes are, from left to right, Jennie Haydock, Betty MacRae (née Jenkinson), Miss Horner, Miss Herdman, Kathleen Draper, Lily Rimmer and Doris Jackson.

Daish's shop, 12 Church Street, 1974. This traditional grocer's shop is remembered fondly by local people. The sides of home-cured bacon hanging in the window show what a vast choice they provided for their customers.

Touring the *Advertiser* office, 1962. The *Ormskirk Advertiser* has brought news to the townsfolk and has served as their voice since 1853. Here a group from the Scottish Society are examining trays of type when they were taken around the printing works. Left to right: Lil Brown, Bill Wilson, Linda Nichol, John Pope, Mary Pope, Caroline Parr, Joan Gibbons and George Naylor.

CHAPTER TWO

PUBLIC SERVICES

The workhouse in Wigan Road, 1900s. The first workhouse in the town was built in 1732 in Aughton Street to cater for the poor from the neighbouring townships. Two years later a second was opened at Moor Street End for the poor from Ormskirk and from several other townships. The Aughton Street workhouse was sold in 1838, when the two were combined here on the site of the present hospital, which still incorporates some of those early buildings. Even today some local people can claim to have been born in the workhouse!

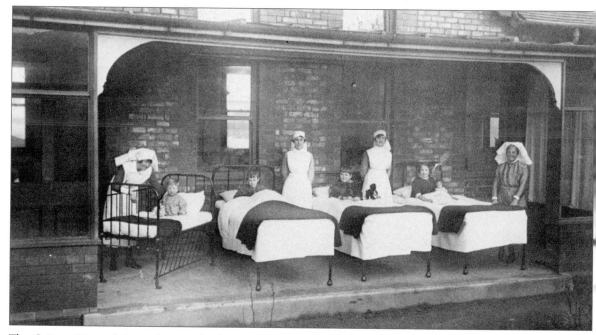

The Cottage Hospital, later the Brandreth Hospital, on Hants Lane. When the hospital was closed the buildings were bought by the Education Authority, who converted it into an adult education centre for Ormskirk College. A tiled mural was rescued from the children's department and installed in the entrance hall of the new hospital building on Dicconson Way.

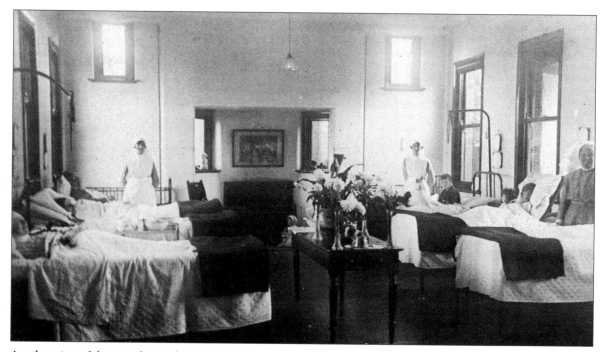

Another view of the same hospital, 1930s. How different the hospital wards are today! At that time patients were given no privacy; even their flowers were bunched together on the central table. Pictures and any reminders of home were cut to the minimum in the belief that by making everything as austere as possible, germs would be eliminated.

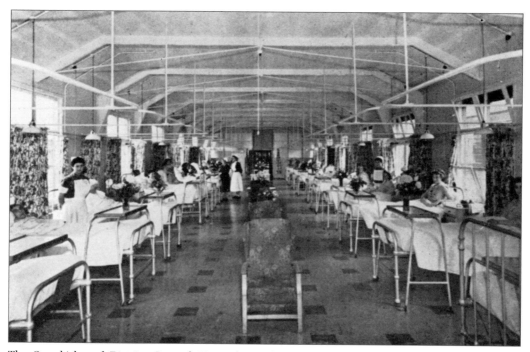

The Ormskirk and District General Hospital, 1950s. By this time ideas had changed. The wards were made more attractive with colourful curtains, easy chairs for those who could get out of bed, and lockers for every patient. Here Matron Helena Lundstrom and nurses Joan Foster and Marion Wall are tending their patients in ward 4, one of the long temporary wooden buildings, known for many years as 'the huts'.

Outside the children's ward. As part of their treatment, children suffering from tuberculosis were nursed in the open air whatever the weather. In this photo Nurse Marjorie Welsh and Nurse Carson are with two of their patients, both of whom seem to be enjoying the photo-call.

The ward for very young children. Nurse Beryl Chapman is seen here caring for one of her patients. Very little had been done to make this ward attractive for the tiny patients. It seems strange to us that no murals had been painted on the walls nor any attractive curtains hung at the windows. I wonder if the children could see those flowers on the top of the partition.

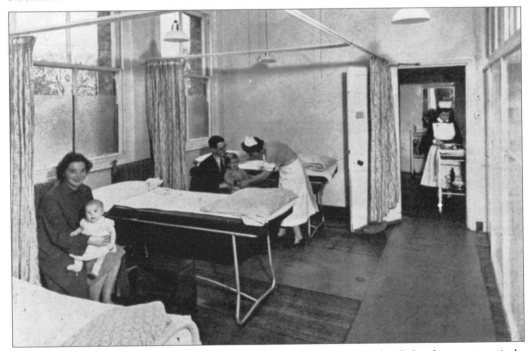

The outpatients' department. A nurse examines a young patient while his father listens attentively, and in the next cubicle a mother and her baby look well and happy. Meanwhile Sister O'Hearne carefully checks the contents of her trolley.

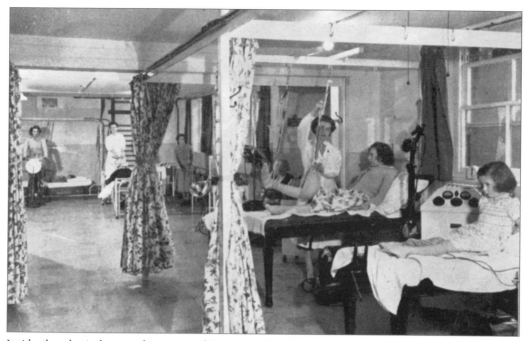

Inside the physiotherapy department. Miss Jones is adjusting some apparatus for a patient, while other aids in use include a cycling machine very similar to those used in fitness gyms today.

Woodholme, one of the nurses' homes. Most nurses lived at the hospital in those days, and so five nurses' homes were provided within the hospital's grounds. The prospectus for the Ormskirk School of Nursing in the 1950s claimed that each bedroom was fitted with central heating and had hot and cold water. The student nurses had access to a sitting room, library and ironing room, and radio and television sets were available for them. All their meals were served in a communal dining room.

At the first hospital garden party, 1956. This was organised by the nurses to raise money for equipment for the hospital. Here are a few of those who were responsible for the huge success of that event. Left to right: Nurses Rosamund Hill, Marjorie Welsh, Muriel Marshall, Mena Davies and a sister midwife.

At the same garden party, which was held behind Fairfield House, another of the nurses' homes. One of the attractions was a comic football match between teams of nurses and other hospital staff. Here Matron is presenting the cup to the winning team. Back row, left to right: -?-, Miss Ryman, -?-, Matron Lundstrom, Pat Anderson, Agnes Nealon, Moira Sullivan, Teresa Fleming. Front row: Miss Jones, two staff from the physio deptartment, Charles Goodwill and Marjorie Welsh.

One of the earliest picture of Ormskirk's fire brigade, when the pump was steam-powered, and the engine was horse-drawn. During the early years of the nineteenth century the fire engine was housed at St Helen's Road alongside the house of the master of the workhouse – now a chemist's shop – on the corner of Wigan Road. Later it was moved into Derby Street to the site of the present Stiles car park.

Another picture of the same crew with the fire engine. Here the crew and their captain, in his peaked cap and gold braid epaulettes, are proudly displaying their equipment, their hoses and hydrant connectors. The setting suggests that they were practising in Coronation Park, and were using the lake as a source of water.

Before the First World War, the fire engine was pulled by Belgian horses from the stables behind the Commercial Hotel. For many years the driver was George Heaton, who is holding the reins in this photograph – dated 1910. The captain of the brigade at this time was Alfred G. Brown (fourth from the left) and his crew were all local volunteers, including Mr Wilding, Mr Cooper, Mr Tom Culshaw, Mr Dick Wignall, Mr Pennington, Mr Stewart, Mr Cooper, Mr Stewart and Mr Martland.

The fire station on the junction of County Road and Aughton Street. Before it was converted into the fire station this building was The Rose Marie, a restaurant and ballroom. It was built in the late 1930s and was requisitioned by the army early in the war. The fire services bought the building in the late 1940s and converted the ballroom into a garage for the engines and the restaurant into offices for the staff. It was an ideal site because it had easy access to so many different routes.

The fire station today. The 'Fire Engine Station' notice on the lawn was moved from the site of the previous fire station in Derby Street.

Devastation after a fire. The helmeted fire crew on p. 38 probably fought this fire at Draper's saw mill on Parr's Lane on 26 October 1915, and prevented further damage. Here Draper's employees have cycled to the site to survey the damage. When steam engines were used in sawmills and timber yards there was always a great risk of fire.

An accident in August 1938. A lorry laden with milk churns travelling south from Rufford swerved to avoid a second lorry carrying coal. It ploughed through a hedge on the corner of Burscough Street and Moss Lane – now Yew Tree Road – and ended up on the front lawn of the home of Major Lyon. Here passers-by are watching the breakdown men trying to move the obstruction.

Constable Keel with his bicycle about to set out
on patrol around Halsall in 1930. The old
police house was behind the post office on
Summerwood Lane.

Two Ormskirk policemen on duty at a traffic accident. This crash at the junction of Knowsley Road
and Ruff Lane occurred in June 1939 when a dairy van and a motorcycle and sidecar collided. The
van can be seen upside down to the left of the picture, and the front of the sidecar has been
smashed beyond recognition.

Another case for the police. Thieves broke into a jewellery shop at 28 Church Street one night in April 1938. They smashed a door panel and stole goods from the window display. When these men were passing on their way to work at 7 o'clock in the morning, they stopped to examine the damage.

When Southport Flower Show was over in August 1938, an AA patrolman was stationed at a busy road junction in Scarisbrick. He had the novel idea of fixing a mirror on to the platform on which he stood, so that he could have a view of the traffic approaching from behind without having to turn round.

Inside Halsall post office, 1909. The postmistress was Mrs Maudsley, seen here beside the switchboard with her son Arthur in her arms. She connected callers and also served any customers who called at the shop. Of course there were very few telephones in the Halsall district at that time.

The inauguration of the *6d* telegram. This was celebrated at Ormskirk in June 1935 when Lady Scarisbrick sent a congratulatory telegram to the Prince of Wales from the head post office in Aughton Street. Afterwards the head postmaster, Mr G.H. Thomas, showed the visitors around the post office. They were, from left to right, Mr C. Marples JP, Sir Thomas and Lady Rosbotham, Mr H. Taylor (Chairman of Ormskirk Urban District Council), Lady Scarisbrick, Sir Everard Scarisbrick and Mr G.H. Thomas. On the far right is one of the post office staff.

Eric Staniforth, the engineer for the Lancashire Electric Power Company which was based in Manchester. The town's original supplier, the Ormskirk Electric Supply Company, was taken over in 1925 by the LEP, which in its turn was absorbed by NORWEB in 1949. The Ormskirk offices were in Park Road on the site now occupied by Safeway's supermarket.

A group of employees from the Lancashire Electric Power Company enjoying a break in the sun. Behind the tennis court are their offices and workshop building, which has the slogan 'Use More Electricity' on the end of the gable. Among the group are Margaret, James and Bill Keating, Mr and Mrs Loukes and Mr and Mrs Brookes.

Inside the waterworks in Springfield Road, Aughton, 1930s. During the Victorian era when this complex was built, the interior of works such as these, their columns, rails and even such details as the racks for the wrenches, were designed with the intention of making the work-place a pleasing environment.

Reflections at the waterworks. The tall ornate chimney was for the smoke from the steam pumping engine. Again, every effort has been made to construct buildings – even those as utilitarian as pumping stations – that were architecturally attractive.

CHAPTER THREE

AGRICULTURE

White House Farm, the home of the Smith family on St Helens Road, Bickerstaffe, c. 1900. The old waterworks on Scarth Hill and the chimney of the pumping engine can be seen in the background. The old pig sties with their flagstone walls, the cart and the bundles of sticks, the pump and slatted table with some kind of a box on it, all create a picture of activity suddenly suspended. Perhaps it was dinner time.

At Harker's Farm on Plex Lane, Barton. After the winter the ground had to be broken up before seed potatoes could be planted. Here Tom Whalley is using a horse plough to break up the ground into ridges in readiness for the manure to be spread into the furrows.

John and Bill Whalley preparing for muck spreading, 1923. The ground had to be well fertilised to ensure a good crop, and at that time manure was the best fertiliser. Many of the fields in Barton were spread with manure brought to the district by canal from Liverpool, where it was collected from the streets and from the city's stables and cow sheds. There were many manure wharves along the canal in Lydiate, Haskayne and Halsall, where local farmers could collect this valuable fertiliser.

These potato pickers had returned to Merridale Farm, not far from the north-western outskirts of Ormskirk, with a wagon full of sacks of potatoes, and were preparing to stack them in the storage sheds. Posing for a photograph gave some of them a welcome chance to sit down and rest for a moment.

During wartime it was difficult to get labour for the harvest. Consequently helpers were sent to farms where they were needed. One of these farms was Hesketh's, and here we see a group of the workers enjoying life in the fields on 27 September 1943.

The West Lancashire potato merchants on their trip to Jersey. As soon as the early potatoes were harvested in Jersey, many of the merchants went to the island to buy a quantity for their customers. As Ormskirk was renowned for its potatoes, many merchants were based in the district, and their association organised the trip. They stayed at the Pomme d'Or Hotel in St Helier, and here they are pictured on the docks waiting for the boat to take them home.

Labourers with a steam engine after threshing at a farm in Bickerstaffe. The soldier standing among the labourers suggests that this picture was taken during the First World War.

Lunch-time for the horses. These animals had been working for several hours and so had been given their nosebags full of fodder. Their backs had been covered to prevent them getting cold while they rested. Meanwhile the work of loading the bales of straw continued.

At Dam Wood Farm in Scarisbrick, 1936. This time it was the turn of the workers to have a rest. The teamsmen and their fellow workers were as follows. Back row, left to right: Tom Ackers, ? Porter, Bob Taylor and Joseph Taylor. Front row: John Ackers, Wilf Taylor and Joe Ackers.

Haymaking on Daniel Draper's farm in Parr's Lane, Aughton. At hay-time all available men were enlisted to help with this very labour-intensive work. Every kind of headwear ranging from a cap to a boater was used to protect the workers from the sun.

Wimbrick Mill. This mill stood at the top of Aughton Brow on the site of Colinmander Gardens. In the early days the sails of the mill were covered with sailcloth made from linen woven locally; in fact Nicholas Blundell of Crosby records in his diary in October 1713 that he bought sailcloth in Ormskirk for his mill. Of course the sails could only produce power when the wind was blowing, and so in the nineteenth century wind power was replaced by the more reliable steam power.

When they were no longer in use the sails were removed from the mill and power from the steam engine was used to turn the grindstones in the mill.

Wimbrick Mill. This mill could be seen from the Mersey and was used by mariners as a navigation point. For many years the owners of the mill were paid by the river authorities to paint it regularly, so that it could be seen more clearly from the estuary. It ceased to operate in 1910.

A group of pea pickers in the fields at Bickerstaffe Hall, 1930s. Several workmen who cannot be identified are standing behind and there are a couple in front with the boys. The pea pickers are, back row, left to right: Lizzie Sumner, -?-, -?-, Mrs Phillipson, Annie Sumner, May Oldfield, Liz Sumner, Ann Marsh, Maggie Harrison, the two Hogarth sisters, -?-, Liza Lowe. Middle row: Jane Speed, -?-, Edith Sumner, Cissie Linch, Mrs Shingler, Hilda Oldfield, Nellie Sumner, Ada Bryers, -?-. In front are three young boys, Bill Phillipson, Bill Sumner and Bill Oldfield.

A load of cabbages on its way to Liverpool market. This team of horses belonging to George Hesketh of Aughton was caught by the camera at the junction of Town Green Lane and Prescot Road. The signpost still stands in the same position, but it has been mutilated almost beyond recognition.

The Mickering. This building was converted into three cottages when the modern farmhouse was built. In the 1930s the cottage on the left housed the teamsman, Harvey, the middle one the cowman, Robinson, and the one on the right Tony Gibbons, the labourer. Here Reuben Baxendale is seen alongside the horse. The two cottages on the left have been demolished, and now the last one is being upgraded. Until the early 1930s the Mickering was farmed by the Hurst family who diversified into the production of Tatti's Crisps, and pioneered the manufacture of dried potatoes during the Second World War.

This lorry dating from the late 1920s belonged to Jim Bond, who farmed Downholland Hall Farm and is sitting in the cab in this photograph.

Horse transport on the A570 in Scarisbrick, 1951. Riding in the cart as it passed Sutch's Farm near Scarisbrick Hall were J. Cropper, R. Glover, W. Britnell and W. Marshall.

CHAPTER FOUR

TRANSPORT

Ready to go for a drive in the trap. Dora Stretch has the whip and her passenger is Polly Barton. I wonder whether those over-sized riding hats stayed in place when the horse began to trot.

Joseph Bradley (1868–1950) operated a cab service for sixty years from Town Green station.

Mr Bradley driving his landau away from Springfield waterworks, 1935. Riding behind him are Mabel and Billy Bailey with their two daughters, Betty and Peggy.

Edwin Bradley at the wheel of his Humber taxicab, 1914. This was the first taxi to operate in Aughton. Mr Bradley used to meet passengers at Town Green station and take them to their homes in the days when few people had their own cars.

The Draper family outside the sawmill in Parr's Lane. Rachel Ashcroft was the lucky one to ride the horse, while the other children, Edward Ashcroft, Daniel Ashcroft, Joseph Draper, Margaret Ashcroft, Margaret Draper, Daniel Draper and Laura Draper, rode in the wagonette.

The Commercial Garage. After the First World War the landlord of the Commercial Hotel – now the Café Bar – on Derby Street was Alfred G. Brown, who also operated this garage in the yard behind the hotel. Earlier in the century he had livery stables in the yard where horses and traps could be hired. The last building on the right, now the workshops of the upholsterers C. Smith & Co., was the harness room and the upper door led into the hay loft. On a seat in the yard is Alfred Brown, and on his left are his driver George Heaton, and his sons Cyril and Stanny.

Lizzie Cave, who used to tell her grandchildren about the day in the 1880s when she watched the first attempt to drive a motor car from Ormskirk to Liverpool.

Advertising Brown's Commercial Garage, 1924.

The funeral of Sam Brighouse. Mr Brighouse was a well-known lawyer, a governor of the grammar school and benefactor of local causes. The driver holding the reins is Cyril Brown from the Commercial Garage and his companion on the box is Mr Constantine. The hearse from the Commercial Garage was always pulled by black horses, usually by the two named Philip and Major.

A trap in front of the gateway to Lathom House, driven by Alfred G. Brown. His passenger is Mr Pinnington, a wine and spirits dealer who toured the public houses of the district collecting orders. Nigger, the horse pulling the trap, was very docile and a great favourite among local children.

Halsall station on the Cheshire Lines Barton branch. This was abandoned as a passenger line long before the Beeching cuts. The station was the scene of great rejoicing on 22 August 1898 when Count Andre de Casteja of Scarisbrick Hall arrived home with his bride, Pauline d'Espeuilles. The station was festooned with banners and a large archway with the words 'Welcome Home' on it was erected over the entrance. On the platform was an official welcoming committee, and children from the local schools lined the route back to the hall.

Town Green station before the electrification of the line on 3 July 1911. At this time it was part of the network operated by the Lancashire and Yorkshire Railway.

Mr Percy Critchley, the stationmaster at Town Green station in the garden in 1922.

Town Green station staff, 1920s. Percy Critchley, the stationmaster, is behind, and on his right is Harry Rotheram, the clerk, while kneeling on his right is Mr Abram. I do not know the names of the other members of the staff.

One of the engines caught in the snow drifts outside Aughton station, 1940s. Several trains including the Scottish express were snowbound and engines were sent from the depot to clear the snow and tow them out. They too became marooned in the drifts and, because they could not get coal to stoke the boilers, the pipes froze, the boilers burst and several engines were completely wrecked.

The bridge over the railway at Aughton Park station. Through the bridge can be seen the workings of the gritstone quarry, where sandstone slabs were also quarried. A steam engine powered the crusher which produced ballast for railway tracks and other uses. After the quarry was abandoned, local youths used to search for 'magic mushrooms' among the debris.

Ormskirk station with the 'Skem Jazzer' in 1912. This type of steam railcar was most unusual as it incorporated the engine and the carriages in one unit. It was very popular for bringing people from the outlying districts around Skelmersdale into the town. Ormskirk was a very busy station at that time when through trains went to Preston and beyond.

Fred Forshaw with two of his workmates at Ormskirk station. How small they look beside one of the huge steam locomotives!

Ormskirk station in its heyday, 1940s. The two platforms connected by a footbridge were fully operational and lines also went into the coal yard on the left.

A young lady with her bike in Stanley Street. Before the introduction of cheap cars cycling was very popular, and almost every town had its cycling club. Cafés catered specifically for these clubs and hung signs for the CTC – Cyclists' Touring Club – outside their premises. These cafés were listed, so that groups could plan their routes to call for refreshments where they knew they would be welcome.

James Smith of White House Farm with his Enfield motorcycle. The bulb horn, the acetylene light and the V-twin cylinder engine were features of this motorcycle, which was first made towards the end of the First World War.

Going on a coach trip: the staff of the *Ormskirk Advertiser* assembled in the town centre. Left to right: Bruce Forshaw, Jim Johnstone, Bill Berkeley, John Forshaw, Fred Hankin, Johnny Holland, George Eastham, Jack Robinson, Bert Staniforth, Bill Rourke, Gerty Georgeson, Sam Rogers, Nellie Dilworth, Olive Forshaw, Florrie Langton, Nellie Forshaw, Nancy Wallbank, Ella Hartley, Ted Ashcroft and Tom Barker.

Burscough Street in the 1950s, before it was pedestrianised. We cannot imagine how two-way traffic and pedestrians could get down such a narrow street. The old shops of Woolworth's, Stokers, the Maypole and Swarbrick's pork butchers – in the distance – can be seen over the traffic.

CHAPTER FIVE

WARS & RUMOURS OF WARS

Colonel Eastham reviewing the Ormskirk troop of the Lancashire Hussars outside the Kings Arms, c. 1900.
These soldiers were recruited locally and were the forerunners of the territorials who were founded in 1903.
Colonel Eastham donated the land on which the Drill Hall – now the Civic Hall – was built in 1899.

Colonel Eastham's home in Southport Road.
All that remains today of this house, near
the Comrades' Club, are the stone gateposts
with the name of the house, Edenfield,
carved on them.

In Colonel Eastham's garden, outside his billiard room. The elderly gentleman sitting in the front of
the group is James Eastham, who was born in 1813 and, as a talented cabinet maker, worked
under Pugin. It is possible that the soldier with the white beard was Sergeant Major Nunnerley,
who survived the charge of the Light Brigade in the Crimean War and acted as drill sergeant for the
Hussars. An interesting local feature is the clay pipe in the hand of the man on the extreme right.
Was it one of the many made in Rainford at that time?

A memorable meeting. These five soldiers, who were the sons of Mrs Bushell (née Bate), landlady of the Railway Hotel in Aughton, enlisted for the army during the First World War and met only once during the four years, in 1918. This photograph, taken at their home, The Cottage, in Prescot Road, commemorates the occasion. Back row, left to right: Sergeant Mo Glover and Joe Bushell. Front row: Tom Glover, Billie Glover and Charlie Bushell.

Hattersley's during the First World War. The factory had been turned over to war work and was making shell cases and other munitions. The girls wore these strange caps to keep their hair away from the machinery, but no guards had been put around the buffing machine to protect the workers from injury.

Lathom Hall. This hall was built to replace the Lathom House that was destroyed in 1645 after the second siege of the Civil War. It was originally the home of the Derby family, who sold it in 1722 to Henry Furnes of London. It passed to the Wilbraham Bootle family, who owned it until the present century. During the First World War it became a remount depot, where horses were trained to serve with the Forces. After the war it fell into ruins, and the only part now remaining can be seen behind the arcades on the right of the picture.

A wartime postcard. The message on the back, from one of the soldiers stationed at Lathom Hall, reads: 'Dear Ernie, This is a photo of the beginning of C. Lines and the Dry Canteen. We are quite well. There is nothing extraordinary going on. Thanks for the cake it was tres bonne. We enjoyed it immensely. I will get you some more cig. cards when I get some. Hope you are all well love from Martin.'

The Joys of Lathom Park.

There's a beautiful spot I'd like to mention,
Where you often hear —Stand at Ease !
Now, do it smart—Attention !
It's eighteen miles from Liverpool, by jove, it's a treat.
No matter where you go or turn,
A woman you seldom meet.

They call it Lathom Park, all bordered round with trees,
The worst of all, is, you can't do what you please,
It's where the A.V. Corps and Remounts have their
    camp,
And mind you, when it's dark, you need your electric
    lamp.
At night time if you are drowsy, and desire a hearty
    laugh,
Just go down to the "Institute" to the "Cinematograph."

At breakfast time each morning,
We wonder what we'll get,
They say it would be bacon,
But it has not turned up yet.
At dinner time again you are thinking of your lot,
But ten-to-one when it is served, the salt they have forgot.

Each night you sleep on straw, just like a herd of cattle,
And if you happen to turn round, your bones are sure to
    rattle.
When you hear Reveille blown
It makes you feel unwell,
You wish that you and Lathom Park
Were right down, deep in Hell.

When the War is over, and we've captured "Kaiser Billy,"
To shoot him would be merciful, and absolutely silly,
Just send him up to Lathom Park,
And we will end his fears.
And let the mules and horses laugh,
While shedding his last tears.
                                            F.J.W.

On the reverse of this poem the soldier has written: 'Dear Frends, Just a line to say I got back all right but work dose not go down so well after 6 days leave, I have been riding today Saturday till I can't sit down so I am going to bed and it is only 6 o'clock.'

Another postcard from Lathom Camp. This had the message: 'This is the Old Chap you where speaking to at Lathom Park.' The 'old chap' also kept his flowers in formation and took a pride in his garden.

Yet another view of Lathom Camp. Private J.E.B., Army Service Corps remounts, F Squadron, 16 Section Lathom Park Camp Ormskirk, wrote: 'Dear Sunshine, Hope you did not expect a letter, Have'nt time for one here. We never stop work not even for a coffee. Well I've been here a week tonight & like it on the whole, but there are lots of unpleasant jobs to be done here as elsewhere still the war's on so must make the best of it. Continued on Peggy's. Kindest regards JEB.'

This photograph of Thomas and Annie Sutton was taken in a studio at the beginning of the First World War, when Thomas had joined up and was about to leave for France. He carried this photograph in his pocket throughout the war to remind him of his sweetheart in Halsall. When he returned from the war the couple married and lived in the white-washed cottage behind the church in Halsall. This crumpled photograph was forgotten until the next generation began to investigate their family history.

Precautions to combat gas attacks against the civilian population. In September 1938 these ARP workers were employed at Skelmersdale town hall to assemble gas masks ready for distribution to civilians.

Further preparations against attack from the air. In October 1938 schoolboys assisted workmen in Skelmersdale to construct an ARP special test trench in the council park. The authorities hoped to persuade civilians to construct similar trenches in their own gardens for use during air raids.

A group of ARP volunteers including ambulance drivers and air raid wardens outside the ambulance station at the Stanley Arms in Aughton. Left to right: Jim Hale, Mr Crewe, Arthur Waterhouse, Jim Sunter, -?-, Miss Ledson, Annie Sawyer, Lil Bower and Bill Higham.

A Polish soldier with Joyce Welsh outside Edge Hill College. During the last war the college was requisitioned for use as a military hospital and this soldier was one of the patients. Joyce's father was the caretaker at the college and so the family lived in the lodge. The young members of the family were great favourites with the soldiers who were so far from home.

Outside St Cuthbert's Church in Halsall. On 28 April 1944 representatives of the forces and various other organisations gathered to attend the United Thanksgiving Service held as one of the events in 'Salute the Soldier' week. During that week special efforts were made to encourage people to support the National Savings campaign.

Number Two Company of the Royal Army Ordnance Corps, 1947. This group of territorials was photographed at the top of Green Lane opposite the Drill Hall – now the Civic Hall on the present car park. The three soldiers who can be named are Captain Tommy C. Roberts, who had earlier served in the Chindits, in the centre, Billy Turner, behind on the left by the gun, and Pim Westhead, third from the left.

YOUNG PEOPLE

Miss Grayson with her pupils at Holt Green School in Aughton, before the First World War. Back row, left to right: Miss Grayson, Ashcroft, R. Prescott, C. Huyton, R. Parr, Bradley. Third row: Ivy Pond, E. Bradley, W. Grantham, W. Kirby, J. Graves, R.A. Draper, A. Foster. Second row: E. Cropper, L. Grantham, R. Hardman, E. Billen, J. Spencer, A. Cropper, A. Skelland. Front row: J. Pope, C. Moore, J. Prescott, A. Flint.

Miss Hare's school on Southport Road, opposite the Comrades Club, between 1910 and 1912. Only a few of the pupils can be named. Back row, left to right: John Olverson, ? Molyneux, ? Vose, -?-, John Molyneux, -?-, -?- Cyril ?, -?-. Third row: May Casey, -?-, -?-, Margaret Banks, Miss Hare, -?-, ? Cammack, -?-, -?-. Second row: Maggie Johnson, -?-, Zita Brown, Miss Hare's niece, ? Cammack, Freda Frapple, Dorothy Banks, -?-, -?-, -?-, ? Frapple. Front row: George Johnson, ? Olverson, -?-, Jack Frapple, -?-, -?-, -?-, Raphie Grundy, -?-.

Another picture of Miss Hare's school, a year or two earlier than the picture above. The back row includes: Cicely Jennings (second from left), Cicely Cammack (fourth from left) and Miss Hare's niece (seventh from left). Middle row, left to right: five unknown individuals, Miss Hare, Miss Frouis, Freda Frapple, Cyril Brown, -?-, -?- (these latter two standing). Front row: -?-, Margaret Banks, -?-, Dorothy Banks, Zita Brown, -?-, Bernard Banks, and four unknown pupils.

The Dickinson family outside their house in Station Road, 1896. The girls wearing those tight wasp-waisted dresses and looking as though they cannot breathe are Emily and Mary. Their two young sisters in their comfortable smocks are May and Beattie. Their mother, Harriet, is also in a tight-waisted dress despite her pregnancy, while the three menfolk resplendent in their watch chains are John H. (their father), George and Chris. The boys in breeches are John W. and Fred. Mr Dickinson used the room on the left as the office for his produce business.

A group of dancers who performed the 'pony dance', 1925. The person at the back is dressed as a jockey. They are, from left to right, Janie Woods, Enid Gardner, Hannah Moorcroft, Mona Ranscombe, Agnes Bushell, Flo Rothwell, May Rothwell, Dorothy Rothwell.

A procession in Burscough Street. The ladies' hats suggest that this was probably taken before the First World War. It is amazing how much time – and expense – was spent by the parents dressing their tiny children for these walking days. They certainly tried to make it a memorable occasion for those taking part. Nevertheless the girls in their sunbonnets and thick black stockings, especially that one biting her finger, look tired of waiting for some action.

The family of Mr Stretch, the auctioneer, about the turn of the century. Standing, left to right: Nelly (who became Mrs Johnstone), Dora (who became Mrs Balmforth), Beatie and Mabel (who became Mrs Phillips). Seated: George, Mrs Stretch (née Mary Barton), Tommy, Mr Stretch and Eva (who became Mrs Birch). The Edwardian dresses of the womenfolk were so elegant but must have been most uncomfortable to wear.

Another procession, again in Burscough Street, late 1920s. The diminutive clergyman and the tiny couple dressed as a bride and groom with their attendants seems to have been a recurring theme in these processions.

Belles of Aughton Morris Dancers in 1925. Back row, left to right: -?-, Jane Woods, Jane Cave, Florence Jackson. Middle row: Edna Johnson, Elsie Sigley, Hannah Moorcroft, Enid Gardner, Eva Rimmer, Dorothy Rothwell, May Rothwell. Front row: Edie Sigley, Sarah Beresford, Edna Foulkes, Sally Light, Flo Rothwell, Beatrice Moorcroft.

The staff and pupils at Miss Bragg's private school in Chapel Street, 1920s. Back row, left to right: Jim Freeman, Phillip Torr, John Balmforth, Harry Freeman, Eric Riding, -?-, Albert Wright. Third row: -?-, Mary Riding, -?-, -?-, Leonard Riding, Joan Daniels, Gladys Jones, Joan Constantine, Dorothy Constantine, Frank Batty, -?-. -?-, Betty Daniels, -?-, -?-. Four unknown scholars are behind the second row. Second row: -?-, Kenneth McCrae, Winifred Berry, -?-, -?-, Miss Bales, -?-, Miss Bragg, -?-, Emma Rosbotham, Margaret Busbridge, Mary Freeman, -?-, Jack Thompson. Front row, sitting on the grass: Barbara Grundy, Mary Holgate, Dick Barry, Mary Garner, -?-, Ruth Esther, Margaret Peet, Jean Young, Timothy Duxfield, Roy Thompson, Hilda Ashcroft, Mary Balmforth, Audrey McCrae, Dorothy Beardswood and Tom Clayton.

St James School, Westhead, 1910. Unfortuneately I have no names for these children or their teachers. I wonder why that one boy was allowed to sit on the tricycle-cum-hobby horse, while his classmates stood around so stiffly in their starched white collars.

A treasured souvenir belonging to Mrs Woods of Bickerstaffe. The school was the centre for the festivities to commemorate the coronation, and no doubt the children played a major role in those celebrations.

Yet another procession, this time in Moor Street. This was either a Sunday School anniversary parade from the parish church or a walk from St Anne's. Certainly the little girls were in their very best clothes – and hats – for the occasion. It is interesting to see a close-up view of Gilbey's wine shop and the offices of Mr Stretch the auctioneer, where Taylor's shop stands today.

Another procession. This time the occasion was St Anne's procession, Aughton Street, August Bank Holiday Monday, 1928. This photo was taken as it passed the Penny Shop and Mr Rose the saddler's – now the site of Safeway's. The garlands were held over the Queen and the Dowager Queen. The girl on the right holding the second garland is Mary Forshaw, and the child at the front with a posy is Celia Spencer. The garlands of fresh flowers must have been heavy to carry around the streets.

Bickerstaffe School, 1922. Back row, left to right: John Rawsthorne, Richard Shuttleworth, Stan Aldred, Tom Rosbothom, -?-, Richard Fallowfield, Will Banks. Third row: Annie Heys, Jane Giblin, Emily Rigby, Martha Latham, Gertrude Rigby, Nell Fallowfield, Ellen Leatherbarrow, Elizabeth Shacklady, Bessie Banks, Annie Smith. Second row: Doris Owen, Nell Spencer, Edith Sumner, Margaret Bimpson, Tabitha Webster, Rene Hearne, Doris Berry, Margaret Orritt. Front row: Harry Dagnall, Will Rimmer, Jim Hodge, Jim Turnock, Jim Bradshaw, Ted Bradshaw, Dick Gaskell, Fred Sumner, Len Rigby, Harry Rigby.

Bickerstaffe School, 1924. Back row, left to right: Len Rawsthorne, Jim Turnock, Dick Gaskell, Will Berry, Will Tyrer, James Bradshaw, Teddy Bradshaw, John Rawsthorne. Middle row: Thomas Houghton, Tom Shacklady, Will Rimmer, James Oldfield, Fred Sumner, -?-, -?-, Harry Rigby. Front row: Peggy Fallowfield, Doris Berry, Tabitha Webster, Rene Hearne, Doris Hesketh, Betty Birchall, Doris Owen, Annie Heys, Margaret Orritt, Deborah Berry, Nell Fallowfield, Emily Rigby, Edith Sumner, Theresa Eccleston, Nell Spencer, Alice Carter, Gwen Brown.

Preparing for Christ Church's annual May Queen ceremony, 10 May 1930. The retiring Queen, Ada Rothwell of Clieves Hill, was adjusting the crown of the Queen Elect, Margaret Sholicar of Cottage Lane, before they left for the crowning ceremony. Holding the trains are their proud mothers – on the left Mrs Rothwell and on the right Mrs Polly Sholicar.

And it rained! The Queen Elect and her retinue were given no shelter from the rain as they entered the field at the corner of Long Lane and Prescot Road. Margaret was elected May Queen by her school fellows at Christ Church School.

Maypole dancers from Bickerstaffe Mission, 1913. Among these dancers from the Girls Friendly Society are Alice Anderton, Dolly Marsh, Mary Alice Peet and her sister.

Strathnaver school in Aughton. The two Miss Gortons ran this school on Town Green Lane nearly opposite the site of the present primary school. Most of the pupils came from the Granville Park area, and they used to give concerts and displays in the Aughton Institute. The Misses Gorton retired before the last war and the house was demolished in the 1940s.

Jenny Ainscough, the first Rose Queen of Halsall School, 1929. Her cousin Peggy Ainscough was chosen to be her attendant, and here they are after the ceremony, taking their new roles very seriously. Perhaps Jenny was having difficulty balancing that huge crown of roses on her head.

Halsall Rose Queen with her attendants after her crowning, 24 June 1933. Back row, left to right: William Wallbank, crownbearer, Mary Gibbons, Margaret Prescott, Robert Scarisbrick, John Ball. Second row: John Knowles, Hilda Knowles, Rose Queen. Front row: Doris Sisney and Winnie Sutton. In those days boys could be persuaded to don silken breeches and white wigs for special occasions.

CROWNING

OF THE

ROSE QUEEN

AND

FIELD DAY:

SATURDAY, JUNE 24th, 1933,

AT 2-30 P.M.,

IN HALSALL PARK

(BY KIND PERMISSION OF MR. D. OSWALD).

Queen - - - - - *MISS HILDA KNOWLES.*

Maids of Honour :
  MARY GIBBONS.
  MARGARET PRESCOTT.
  DORIS SISMEY.
  WINIFRED SUTTON.

Herald :
  ROBERT SCARISBRICK.
Crown Bearer :
  WILLIAM WALLBANK.

Pages :
  JOHN BALL.
  JOHN KNOWLES.

Programme - - - Price 2d.

T. HUTTON, *Advertiser* Office, Ormskirk

A souvenir belonging to one of the maids of honour.

The choir from Halsall School, 1930. Although they normally had no uniform, the girls wore gym slips on this occasion, when they competed at Blackpool Musical Festival. Back row, left to right: Peggy Clare, Ernest Grimshaw, Richard Haslam, Clifford Waites, Tommy Shacklady, Eddie Sergeant, Ronnie Townsend, John Banks, Joan Gradwell, -?-. Middle row: Margaret Sergeant, Muriel Barton, Peggy Shacklady, Mildred Johnson, Lily Shacklady, Winnie Sutton, Dorothy Carr. Front row: Doris Aspinall, Freda Witter, Edna Sharrock, Peggy Ainscough, Kathleen Townsend, Peggy Marshall and Freda Bradley.

Doris Sisley, Helen Taylor and Winnie Sutton picking crocuses behind the churchyard in Halsall in the days when children were allowed to pick wild flowers wherever they wanted.

The teachers at Derby Street School, early 1930s. Back row, left to right: Miss Peet, Miss Tyrer, Miss Tittershill (later Mrs Baty), Miss Rooks, Miss Sephton, Miss Howard. Front row: Miss Mansell, Mrs Rimmer, Miss Taylor (headmistress), -?- and Miss Pilkington.

Prizewinning babies at Lathom Women's Institute annual show, 8 September 1938. Left to right: Clive Butterworth (9–12 months section winner), Maureen Wilding (3–6 months), Patricia Wood (6–9 months), Barbara Vincent (3 months).

The athletics team from Aughton Street School in 1936, when they won the Blundell Cup at the district sports held in the field opposite the Council Offices. After winning the Cup almost every year, they were allowed to retain it. Later it was offered for competition among junior schools. Back row, left to right: Stanley Lea, Toot Winrow, Geoff Rimmer, Les Ball, Wilf Snape, ? Moorcroft. Middle row: George Twist, ? Cheetham, Ronnie Booth, Sidney Sarbutts, George Glover, Fred Parker. Front row: Houghton, ? Foster, Bill Crompton, John King, Gerald Ashcroft, Francis Ashcroft. The teacher standing behind is Eric Soar.

Ormskirk Girl Gymnasts with their instructor Miss Smith at Ormskirk Senior School, Wigan Road, 17 June 1939. Today's gymnasts would be horrified if they were expected to perform in this kind of tunic.

At the Victoria Baths in Southport, July 1938. These boys ranged on the diving boards won their races at Aughton Street Boys' School's annual swimming competition. Mr Hunter, their headmaster, is on the left, and one of the judges, Mr Wilfred Mahood, the District Scout Commissioner, is on the extreme right. The three teachers standing under the boards are Mr Soar, Mr Batey and Mr Hesketh.

Demolishing part of the old Senior Girls' Elementary School in Wigan Road, 1938. In 1937 plans were made to transfer the senior boys from Aughton Street School to the Wigan Road School. The old building had to be extended to accommodate the boys, and so the opportunity was grasped to modernise the whole complex. Although the senior boys' and girls' schools were combined in the same building, the children were separated into single sex classes. The extensions were completed in 1938 at the cost of £26,000.

This photograph of Ormskirk Grammar School's First Hockey Eleven appeared in the local paper on 23 March 1939. Back row, left to right: M. Cropper, M.E. Rimmer, B. Gardiner, A. Eckersley, M.D. Furst. Middle row: E.E. Jones, E. Hall (captain), Miss M.E. Brash, F.I.E. MacRae, E.F. Marsh. Front row: E.D. Jackson and M.J. Robertson.

Tower Troupe of morris dancers. This parade took place in 1953, and here the troupe are shown on Moor Street as they approach Stanley Street. They had passed the statue of Disraeli which can be seen in the background. The Institute is behind the trees, and the low building is a pair of old cottages which were derelict for years. At the back of the cottages was Hesketh's vehicle repair workshop.

The 1st Ormskirk Guides on the Grammar School field behind the houses in Altys Lane, 1943. Back row, left to right: Pat Smith, Beryl Yarwood, Grace Balmer, Annie Edge, Hazel Johnson, Jean Davidson, Marjorie Bellingal. Third row: Ruth Moore, Jenny Taylor, -?-, Pat Dean, Rosemary Jackson, Winnie Yates, -?-, Jean Bolton, Margaret Scragg, Mabel Whittier, Rita Spalding, Pat ?, -?-, -?-, -?-. Second row: Rita Yarwood, -?-, -?-, Patsy Jowett, Jean McDougal, Brenda Woods, Brenda Grayson. Front row: -?-, Sheila Maher, Jean Rosbotham, Margaret Edge, -?-, Jean Whittle.

Mr Glayzer with Class 3A 1 at Greetby Hill School, 9 May 1956. In 1973 he, his wife and daughter Andrea were victims of the Summerland fire on the Isle of Man. Back row, left to right: Irene Roberts, Janet Ellison, Jim Hesketh, Brian Hignet, John Palmer, June Fowell. Fourth row: Barry Kirk, Alan Robinson, Derek Huyton, David Watt, Michael Thomas, David Taylor, Rodney Rasburn, Peter Freeman. Third row: Jean Lyon, Angela Sheekey, Katherine Sharp, Linda Bilton, Jane Laurenson, Barbara Smith, Susan Gregson, Pam Stetch, Pat Roberts. Second row: Kevin Clayton, Donald Spur, Gary Lyon, Gerald Walker, John Sumner, Harry Pennington, Geoffrey Howard, Billy Young. Front row: Pat Oldfield, Jean Staniforth, Dorothy Beadle, Irene Berkley, Janet Sewell, Mary Chatterton, Linda Oldfield, Pam Helsby and Dorothy Foster.

Another group of Girl Guides from Ormskirk. At the back, left to right: Moira Griffin, -?-, Beryl Abram, -?-, -?-, Marion Lily, -?-, Thelma Caldwell. Middle row: Joyce Taylor, -?-, Rosemary Crowe, Phoebe Chapman and, slightly behind, Pam Griffin and Jeanette McCrae. Front row: Cheryl Haskayne, Margaret Aldcroft and Joan Aldcroft.

The staff at Ormskirk County Secondary School, 1960s. Back row, left to right: Frank Fletcher, Charles Fogg, Gillie Houghton, Percy Hender, Bill Mitton, Charles Phillips, Ken Lowe, Tom Roberts, Mr Nelson. Seated: Mr Anderton, one of the secretaries, Harold Weston, Miss Holmes (another secretary), Mr Ellison (the headmaster), Richard Thomas, Mrs Fawcett, Wilfred Corfe and Mr Lowe.

In a classroom at Hants Lane School in 1960. Playing the xylophones are, at the back, Christine Wright, -?-, Patricia Kidman. On the front row: -?-, Diane Taylor, Angela Coleman, Barbara Tolmie.

Crowning the statue of the Virgin on the site of the St Anne's Social Centre, 1963. Those taking part are, left to right, Margaret Fagin, Sheila Brighouse, Marie Fitzpatrick, -?-, Patricia Tolmie (who was to crown the statue), and Jim Howard (who carried the crown). In front are Janice Livesey and Christine Rainford.

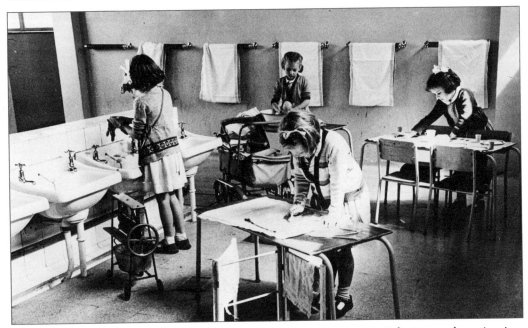

Learning domestic science, Greetby Hill School, early 1950s. Patricia Roberts was busy ironing, Jean Lyon was laying the table, while Irene Roberts was bathing the baby. I cannot name the girl washing the clothes.

CHAPTER SEVEN

EVENTS & LEISURE ACTIVITIES

An advertisement for the third show organised by the Aughton, Lydiate and Maghull Horticultural, Poultry & Pigeon Society, 1894.

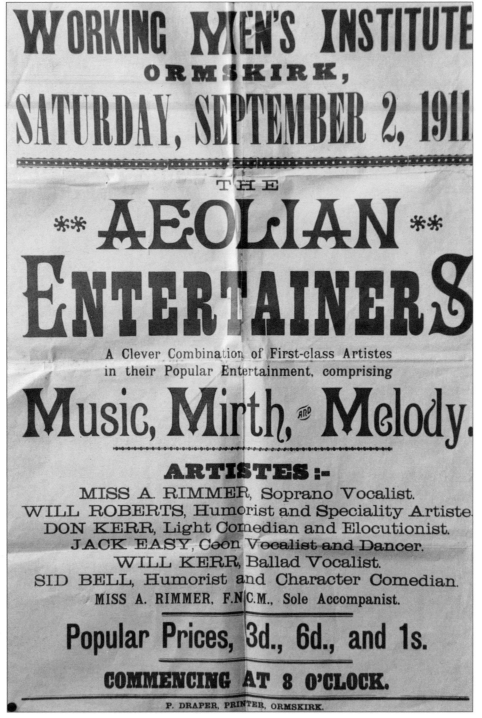

This advertisement speaks for itself. The Working Men's Institute stood on Moor Street on the site of the bus station and was the venue for all kinds of entertainments and celebrations. It is interesting that the bill was printed by P. Draper, whose descendants still have a stationer's shop in Burscough Street, where this bill was printed in 1911.

The Aeolian Concert Party, 1913/14. Seemingly they had acquired two more female artists in the two years since the playbill, and no doubt in the coming war years they would have to rely even more on the talents of the womenfolk. I wonder if the artists, most of whom came from the Ormskirk district, are the same as those listed on the playbill two years earlier.

This crowd of ladies had gathered for some great occasion at Halsall Church, but what that was is a mystery. Certainly from the style of their dresses, it must have taken place in the early years of the twentieth century before the First World War, long before the lych gate which is now so familiar to us was constructed.

A coach outing from Bickerstaffe Mission. Back row, left to right: Jim Johnson, Joseph Johnson, Peter Parr, Bert Johnson, Harry Phillipson, -?-, Sam Appleton, Jack Foster, Gem Anderton. Middle row: Richard Sumner, Richard Anderton, Bill Woods, Will Selsby, -?-, Jim Campbell, Mr Turner, Charles Rigby. Front row: Mrs Hesketh, Elizabeth Sumner, Ada Rigby, Nellie Woods, Bob Aspinwall, -?-, Mary Campbell, Annie Turner, Mrs Anderton.

The choirs of both St Michael's Church and of Christ Church, Aughton, on an outing to the Dukeries, 1914. Back row, left to right: the Rev. E. Pickthall, A. Johnson, A. Morris, D. Draper, E. Draper, J. Kirby, J. Draper, Rachel A. Draper, Robert Draper, E. Warlow, Samuel Lake. Third row: G.F. Watts, Miss Clamp, Miss E. Hutton, Miss O. Hutton, William Rothwell, Miss D. Kirby, Miss M. Rothwell, Miss E. Seddon, Miss Hutton, -?-, R. Mitchell. Second row: W. Rothwell junior, T. Rimmer, R. Evison, J. Taylor, R. Lea, J. Mawdsley, J. Sephton, L. Nottingham. Front row: E. Carr, -?-, A. Mitchell, John Draper, Brian Meredith, J. Nixon, John Lake.

Lathom Park Cricket Club, 1910. Back row, left to right: H. Hall, J. Dean, T. Glover, the Rev. A. Score, J. Little, R. Draper, J. Seddon. Front row, seated: ? Bush, J. Moss, B. Ashton, Lord Lathom and the Rev H.H. Hall.

The Ormskirk Ladies Cricket Team in the Pavilion, 1920s. Back row, left to right: W. Stretch, J. Glover, Miss C. Martin, ? Lockin (the pro. with a straw hat), H. Carr, J. Martin, R. Pilkington, J. Pilkington, M. Woods, C. Woods, B. Collinson, M. Cook, J. Hulley, E. Gardiner, A.R. Gardiner. Front row: J. Close, Miss H. Shaw, Miss C. Poole, Miss W. Warlow, Miss M. Jowett, Miss V. Stretch (captain), Miss H. Wilson, Miss E. Jowett, Miss D. Hulley, Miss Bradshaw, Miss Hurst, Miss M. Hulley.

Ormskirk Town Band in the early 1930s. The musicians in this picture include Tom Horner, Mr Sigley and Mr Fazakerley.

Halsall Football Team, 1935. This club, formed in 1919, was a member of the Southport & District League. In the season 1928/9 they won the Colonel White Cup, in 1931/2 the Victory Cup, and in 1935/6 the Senior Charity Cup. One of their members, J. Pears, eventually joined Sheffield United and became a well-known footballer. Back row, left to right: T. Sutton (trainer), J. Rimmer, T. Riley, R. Lamb, W. Knowles (captain), W. Forshaw, J. Blundell, J. Park. Front row: J. Bond, J. Kirby, T. Threlfall, James Thompson, John Thompson.

Ormskirk Cricket Team, the 1st XI, 1936. Back row, left to right: Josh Ainscough, E. Ashcroft, L. Wells, J. Robinson, R.H. Taylor, ? Whitehead. Front row: A. Crompton, R.L. Moorby, M.S. Woods, M. Ainscough, W. Robinson, J.W. Moorby.

The Oddfellows in Halsall, 1937. They had gathered alongside their decorated lorry outside the Saracen's Head before joining the procession to celebrate the coronation of King George VI. On the lorry: Agnes Prescott, Mary Prescott, Jennie Knowles, Nellie Prescott, Mary Knowles, Hilda Knowles and children. Standing, left to right: Edward Banks, John Rimmer, William Gradwell, Charles Shacklady, Robert Draper, Arnold Blundell, Thomas Sutton, -?-, William Gradwell (nephew of his namesake), David Swift, -?-, Thomas Elliot, John Knowles, John Gradwell, Harry Knowles, John Ackers, Stanley Draper, -?-.

A pre-war darts team at the Scarisbrick Arms, Halsall. Back row, left to right: Bill Knowles, Jack Wilson, ? Longton, Thomas Sutton, Harry Whittaker, -?-, George Porter, ? Carr, ? Blundell. Front row: -?-, Arthur Draper, George McCoy, Harry Dickinson, -?-, ? Houghton, -?-, Josh Sutton.

St Anne's Hockey Team, late 1930s. Back row, left to right: John Westhead, Father Steven, Leo Wills, Tom Latham, Tom Moran, Bert Ball. Second row: Frank Moran, Frank Wills, Father Coyle, ? Moorcroft, Jim Culshaw. Front row: Edward Holcroft and Andrew Tolmie.

Robert Mayer with his model of Bickerstaffe church, made completely out of matchsticks, in the early 1940s.

Bellringers from around the district, who had gathered at Christ Church, Aughton, in the 1940s. Left to right: Thomas Rothwell of Aughton, Peter Harvey of Aughton, who had rung for over fifty years, -?-, Peter Crook senior from Blackburn, Captain Jones from Cottage Lane Mission, Jack Brown the churchwarden, Eric Cook from Standish, the Rev. Percy Hobson of Christ Church, -?-, Lester Gray of Liverpool St Michael's, Peter Crook junior, John Rothwell of Aughton and Karen Whyte.

From a newspaper of 18 November 1938. Mr Giles Sharrock was a well-known pigeon fancier of Haskayne, near Ormskirk, seen here with the three gold cups he had won for pigeon racing. He broadcast a talk on pigeon racing in the radio series 'Spotlight on Sport'.

Another interesting item from a newspaper of 17 January 1939. 'Miss Ormskirk' was chosen at a dance in the Ormskirk Institute by Miss Mersey, seated second from the left. The title was awarded to Miss Doris Wright (seated third from the left) and behind are the other competitors. During the middle years of this century it was thought to be an honour to be chosen as a beauty. Nowadays attitudes have changed, and it is thought to be degrading to enter such a competition.

A dart team at the Blue Bell in Barton, 1948. Back row, left to right: Charles Balmer, Joe Cropper senior, Jim Carr (known as Nim), Tom Sephton, Harry Raw (the landlord), Joe Cropper junior, Mrs Raw, Jim Fazakerley, Ken Gaskell, Doris Balmer, Eddie Core. Front row: Jack Higson, Jack Draper, Ted Aindow, Albert Ashton, John Whalley and Tommy Church.

A large group of members of the Catholic Young Men's Society, 1954. They are gathered around the shrine of Our Lady on the site of St Anne's Social Centre. In the centre of this group, wearing surplices, are Peter Latham, Father Teeley and John Ashurst. Behind them on the right are Father Mark Ackers and Father Armstrong.

Ormskirk Horticultural and Chrysanthemum Society show, 1950s. Admiring the blooms are Vic Smith, George Allen and William Potter, who was secretary of the society.

The Young Wives from the parish church with friends on their outing to the Wedgwood Factory, 1950s. Back row, left to right: Mrs Taylor, Mrs Robinson, -?-, -?-, -?-, Mrs Dawson, Mary Allen, driver. Third row: all unknown. Second row: Mrs Griffiths, Mrs Tunks, Mrs Cobham, Mrs Murray, -?-, Mrs Pilling. Front row: Mrs Neill, Mrs Roughley, Mrs Berkley, Mrs Blackburn, Miss Roughley, Mrs Spurr, Mrs Briscoe.

Wilf Burton's Dance Band, 1950s. They were playing for a dance in the Institute, and Mr Heys was the MC. The musicians were, from left to right, Ernie Heyes, Frank Bradley, Jack Edge, Bert Linguard, Wilf Burton and Gus Disley.

An exhibit at the first exhibition given by Ormskirk Flower Club, December 1963. Mrs Peggy Waugh is showing the display to two young visitors, one of whom looks rather doubtful about that squirrel.

Piping in the Haggis at the Burns Supper, 1967. Piper Donald Stewart leads the procession into the Guide Headquarters in Moorgate. Carrying the haggis is Diane Wilson, and behind are Angela Wilson, Katrina Parr, George Naylor and David Robinson. John Pope watches from the doorway.

THE CHANGING LANDSCAPE

A view of old Halsall. The building with the castellated roof and belfry was the old Church of England school, built when the original school-room in the church building became overcrowded with pupils. When the school moved to the present building in 1904 the old school was used for all kinds of social events. It was demolished after the war, and Georgian-style houses were built on the site. The post office under the trees remains enclosed by that same stone wall today.

A cottage on New Street, Halsall. This cottage was about to be demolished in 1985 when this picture was taken. Behind is the more convenient bungalow built to replace it, further away from the traffic on the road to Southport.

Wigan Road, Westhead, c. 1905. The Halton Castle inn can be seen in the centre distance of the picture as the road turns to the left. Most of the cottages on the right have been demolished, while those on the left have been modernised. Porches have been added, and pebbledash and rough-cast rendering have altered the appearance of many of them. The telegraph poles have been replaced by tall street lights.

Mrs Rothwell cycling in Holt Green, *c.* 1936. The children from the school nearby spent their pennies at the shop on the corner of Brookfield Lane – then known as Pudding Street. This was because the farmer's wife at the end of the lane sold black puddings made from the blood of the pigs from the piggery alongside the shop. Jack Carter had the shop until the last war when he converted it into living accommodation. A previous shopkeeper had such a reputation for keenness that it was said she would cut a raisin in half to be certain that the weight was correct.

The same view when the cottage was being demolished in the 1960s. For many years it was the home of Mr Lake, the cobbler, who repaired shoes in the building at the side. The cottage was built in 1744, but no effort was made to preserve it and a little bit of old Aughton was lost forever. The trees were victims of the great storm in 1986, and all that remains now are two stumps covered with ivy.

Ivy Cottage, Black Moss Lane, Aughton. Before the Second World War this cottage had very low ceilings, in fact the grandfather clock stood in a hole 2 ft deep excavated in the floor. The kitchen had one cold tap over a shallow sandstone sink, and the water closet was down the garden. Only the two downstairs rooms – not the kitchen – were lit by gas lights, and a steep winding staircase led up to two small bedrooms which were under the eaves. Mrs Bentham, who rented the cottage for *2d* a week, is seen here with Mrs Prescott and an unknown friend.

The old rectory in Church Lane, Aughton. The original part of this building, including the impressive staircase, was built in the early eighteenth century, but it was demolished in the 1960s. Now the memory of it is preserved in the street name of Old Rectory Green, a group of stylish residences surrounded by trees.

Aughton Street in the late nineteenth century. The George and Dragon (the sign is to the right of the lamp post) was on the corner of Aughton Street and Church Street, and later the site was developed as a bank. Now it is the offices of the Halifax Building Society. Henry Brown's became Rigby Swift's – now Conlon's, the optician, while Lambert's became Balmforth's – now the Cancer Research charity shop. Arrowsmith's, the cooper's workshop (the small building with barrels on the pavement) later became Garside's – now Woolworth's.

An amusing advertisement for Ablett's shoes before the shop moved into Moor Street.

The fishstones in Aughton Street. Across the pavement are the shops of Williams the outfitter, and of Ablett's the shoemaker, and also the entrance to the vet's office. In the seventeenth century Ormskirk court leet compelled fishmongers to sell fish from these stones on market days, and on several occasions fishmongers were fined heavily for leaving 'stinking fish' nearby. In 1808 Thomas Taylor, an early Methodist evangelist, used the stones as a platform when he preached in Ormskirk, long before the first Methodist church was built.

Church Street, during the First World War. Wood's the chemist's can be seen on the corner behind the horse and cart. That building still projects from its neighbour; in fact the building line has persisted since the seventeenth century when some of Lord Derby's tenants were fined for encroaching on to the roadway, and were charged extra rent for the land they had purloined. The stone quoins on the adjoining building, probably another of the encroachments, date its construction to the Georgian period.

An unusual view down Church Street with the clock tower in the distance. A delivery cart with an awning over its load is passing the public house known as the Snigs Foot, and a funeral cortège is approaching the church. Church Street widens towards the front of the photograph, and that old building line also persists today as Tesco's and the neighbouring property have wider pavements than Scotts and the shops nearer to the clock tower.

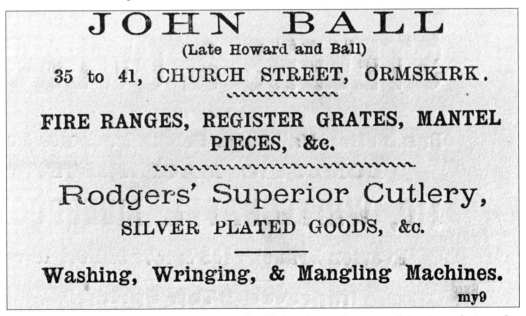

JOHN BALL

(Late Howard and Ball)

35 to 41, CHURCH STREET, ORMSKIRK.

FIRE RANGES, REGISTER GRATES, MANTEL PIECES, &c.

Rodgers' Superior Cutlery,

SILVER PLATED GOODS, &c.

Washing, Wringing, & Mangling Machines.

my9

An advertisement from 1893 for the products of Ball's foundry in the centre of the above photograph.

Moor Street with the King's Arms and Wainwright's ironmonger's shop at the end of the nineteenth century. Shortly after this photograph was taken Wainwright's moved and the shop became the Corn Exchange. The façade of that building was plastered and covered with Tudor-style beams, and a glass canopy was installed to protect the farmers who gathered there. The wide entrance alongside the inn was for carriages and wagons to enter the inn yard.

The market in Moor Street. Although the market is held in the same place today, there are no tables or stalls without awnings nowadays. I wonder how far the owner had pushed that hand cart to bring his goods to market, or perhaps he had a pony which he had stabled in the yard behind the Ship. On the right of Moor Street can be seen Pooley's printing works with the bay window, the offices of Idle and Stretch, the auctioneers, and the glass canopy over the Corn Exchange.

The Catholic Young Men's Society building. This was demolished to make way for St Anne's Social Centre: it was originally the old chapel of St Oswald built in 1785. When St Anne's Church was built, it was converted into a school, as it continued for many years. Then, when the school moved to Hants Lane, it served as a social centre. During the Second World War the upstairs rooms were used by the army, while functions such as dances and whist drives were held downstairs. Originally a row of small cottages stood in front of it on the side of St Anne's Road.

Aughton Street school. This is the only photograph I have been able to find of the boys' school which originally stood adjoining the site of the new bypass, Park Road East. The broken windows show that demolition had already begun, and another of Ormkirk's old landmarks was about to disappear. This boys' school moved to Wigan Road to combine with the girls' school as Ormskirk Senior School (now Cross Hall High) in 1938 (see page 95).

The statue of Disraeli in its original place at the junction of Moor Street and St Helen's Road. The building with the pediment is the Working Men's Institute and Cocoa Rooms – or the Institute as it was known. Local people have happy memories of amateur dramatic or operatic performances or dances held in that building.

Evans and Ball's premises in Burscough Street. There is a pleasing symmetry about the buildings erected in the late eighteenth or early nineteenth century. The upper floors resemble those of Georgian residences, and it is tempting to speculate that at one time this had been a stylish residence before being converted into commercial premises. The central archway allowed access for horse-drawn vehicles to the back of the building. This firm of provision dealers was founded by Joseph Ball, a local preacher and a great worker for the Methodist Church.

Moor Street. In the 1970s Clucas's seeds and garden shop dominated that part of the road.

Moor Street, 1970s. Wenk's flower and vegetable shop served Ormskirk for many years. Their plants and flowers and much of their produce were grown locally at their nursery in Brook Lane. Morrison's travel agents was a more recent arrival in Ormskirk, and is also remembered by the townsfolk, this time for organising many a departure to sunnier climes.

Now we too must depart from these memories, resolved that in our turn we will preserve mementoes and photographs of the present day for the enjoyment of future generations.

ACKNOWLEDGEMENTS

I would like to thank all the many people who have helped me to compile this book. Unfortunately it is impossible to mention all your names within the limits of these pages. Nevertheless my grateful thanks to all of you, to those who have lent me their precious photographs, some which appear in the book, and the many others which had to be rejected because there was not sufficient space to include them; to those who have named the people in the groups for me and to those who have supplied me with the most interesting information, again some of which appears in the book and some which had to be omitted for want of space. Thank you for sparing the time to share your memories with me and with all the readers who, I am sure, will enjoy reading about them.

Finally my thanks to Heaton, my husband, without whose help and expertise with both the camera and the computer this book would never have been completed.

BRITAIN IN OLD PHOTOGRAPHS

SUTTON'S PHOTOGRAPHIC HISTORY OF TRANSPORT

To order any of these titles please telephone our distributor, Littlehampton Book Services on 01903 828800